moon
JOURNAL

CPSIA information can be obtained
at www.ICGtesting.com
Printed in the USA
LVHW100538121218
600165LV00021B/1348/P

9 781979 115599